THE GLASS ENCLOSURE

The Glass ENCLOSURE

IAN POPLE

1996

Published by Arc Publications
Nanholme Mill, Shaw Wood Road
Todmorden, Lancs. OL14 6DA

Design by Tony Ward
Printed at Arc & Throstle Press
Nanholme Mill, Todmorden, Lancs

ISBN 0 900072 00 9

ACKNOWLEDGEMENTS
Some of these poems have appeared in *Arvon/ Observer International Competition Anthology* 1987, *Fiddlehead* (Canada), *Honest Ulsterman*, *Leading Light*, *London Review of Books*, *Oxford Poetry*, *PN Review*, *Poetry Review*, *Poetry Wales*, *Times Literary Supplement*, and *Verse*.

Cover Lino Cut by Wendy Raphael

To O.M. and W.B.P.

The Publishers acknowledge financial assistance from Yorkshire and Humberside Arts Board and North West Arts Board

Contents

THE TREE-LINE

There was the smell of water
sprayed in the late afternoon.
She stood on the other side of the road
looking up at pigeons, as if
scenting the air like a dog.

There had been cries coming
from the cloisters above the tree-line.
Sounds in a language that,
in their separate lessons,
they had only just learned.

For him everything was changed;
he was the lover with a Casaubon tic.
Fascinated by her face, in his mind,
in the quiet house, he touched her body.
Looking out over the sea and holding

in his head those blues and golds
that cameras hold, as under ice
the calm trout waits for its displacements,
he wanted to run out amongst the shining cars,
rain beating on him from all sides.

BASLE

to A.P.

Behind me the garden descends to water.
Each night a balloon drifts over the river,
gas jets stain the silence
and trout rise into the shadows.

I watch the children through curtains
and weariness; this is the other weather,
a new carpet is laid, and the dogs run towards me
over gravel paths. 'No matter who it is

death is all these things and a release.
You know in all those years I only ever
changed trains there, once, in the middle
of the night.' Feet that keep on disappearing

as we walk towards the corner.
You stand beside the table.
As I put back the books I get that
faint childhood smell of snow and urine.

WHEN THE SAINTS

I

I was always killing something
on that road. First a rabbit.
Then a thrush flew up
into the windscreen. I had forgotten
the biology of Britain; that we, too,
have the pine marten and wild orchids.

I was like a freed songbird.
The road ran beside a swollen river
and flooded fields. I was looking for
that familiar spire lit by sudden sun;
the ingenuous smile you give me
as you turn to look out on the carpark.

We complete this room, your rationality
and mine merge and fill it up. My father
is getting as small and as brittle
as the memory of what they told me
was the Great North road. We huddled
in my father's Morris and tall trees bent

over the road as the grey tarmac
dissolved into sunlight. Like
Russ Tamblyn cinematically miniaturised
as Tom Thumb, with his little Irish friends
dancing among the trees, St Vitus
has my father in the palm of his hand.

II

Behind the screen of fields
a film of clouds rolls endlessly.
Even waterfowl fly up

against the swell of the hill,
over the roofs, the tarmac
and the seamless exhaust.

The clouds are tarnished
underneath. The water
does not weigh enough

for simple precipitation.
The gamey tang of horses
crops his turf. The feet

of ducks never quite draw
parallel with the surface
of his canals. This mixture

of exfoliation and impediment:
deafness, St Vitus' Dance,
the pacemaker. As if I

were the missing top joint
from the finger of his right hand
to show where once I might have been.

AMNIOSIS

Only that previous evening all his desperation
had come to her as she climbed into bed,

hoping this other would be asleep.
And they had woken in the no-light

to a disposition of lines that led them
through the day; an old emptiness

from the time before he died. She saw
oilcans on the river, the pattern of sunlight

over leaves, soft mouthings that clouds make.
In the library two girls ate chocolate by a window

until a loud man made them stop and stare,
and she returned home to a stale enquiry into security.

He said 'I'd like to look out on that field
and see an animal, you know. A squirrel, say.

Birds you see them all the time.'
And then they danced great blazing marks where their feet

and sticks rubbed the floor, all that clapping
of hands, and choking on sighs; and burst out

into summer evening and sunlight cut
by the corner of a door, an aircraft grazing the sky.

THE BIG HOUSE

I

As I spake unto you at that time saying
I am not able to bear you, myself alone,
the hand of the mason was taken and led

out into corridors of air, as much as
his feet shuffled over the paving stones
which are brought down and fallen

but we are made strong and stand upright.
On the Chapterhouse, Mr Gill's perspective
has shortened to an estuary where both eyes

move to a single side of the face.
The Christ Child is exposed to fumes
from Corporation Street and Deansgate.

St George genuflects and pouts at the Virgin.
St Denys in his mitre extends a finger
along his crozier towards the Hidden Gem.

'A bad site and an uncouth façade.'
Arm in arm with Pevsner, Pugin walks
inside, 'This building shows to what depths

even good men fall when they go whoring
after strange styles.' Our Lady of Manchester
is anorexic; souls have whistled

through her rib cage since the dawn of time.
They gather on the roof in Lowry's painting
and form the skyline into a set of candles.

Lowry's candles burn with a dark flame.
Souls have gathered in premonition of the Lord
to haunt Our Lady for the rest of her life.

II

A table laid for the Passover; four glasses
of wine drunk leaning to the left,
and one glass for Elijah the Prophet;
and four questions answered by us all
to distinguish this night from all
other nights where we might eat any species

of herb but on this night only bitter herbs
in remembrance of the bitter life of exile.
On all other nights we do not dip even once
but on this night twice of the nuts mixed with wine
as the loam mixed with straw for bricks
for the Pharoah; the shank-bone and the egg

of eternity, slightly burned; the front door
opened to let Elijah in to sip the wine
but it was Kossacks and the curt smell
of frightened horses and my brothers
and my father – shops with no glass
but shutters and iron rods not in streets

but big courtyards with iron gates –
so I could see them breaking off the rods
to fight the Kossacks but the Kossacks
were shooting and I was there and I saw them
shooting a man killed in front of me
on that Coronation Day about the hour

of Solemnity when the Holy Son was sacrificed
to the Father when they began in the city
of Manchester to sacrifice the Jews
to their father – the Devil. And so great
was the delay with this celebrated mystery
that the holocaust could scarcely be finished

on the second day when Hugh of Lincoln
and the Jews alike were sticked like a swine
and first came out the thick, thick blood
and then came out the thin stream of red apples
placed upon a tray for her Lady Maistry
who waits for little Hugh at mass then walks

down to the Jew's garden and the gathering
of echoes beside the fifty fathom well
where the bells of Jewish Emancipation
are rung without men's hands and the books
of Jewish Emancipation are read without
men's tongues and Rose Berman shall walk out

with the gentile merchant seaman
from the other side of Magnolia Street
and they ran a bazaar on Cheetham Hill
and delivered the stuff to Red Bank where the stench
was terrible even though we had cars to go round,
but to go to Red Bank … Does it still smell?

III

They had a lake in Trafford Park
and if it was fine on a Sunday
it used to be packed with people.
They used to walk to it, of course,
most of them. They had piano accordians
and ukeleles and all sorts going on,
it used to be great. There was

rowing boats and an island in the middle,
it was fantastic. In 1926 we went
to Blackpool for the week. My mother
used to scrimp and scrape and I was lucky.
Many children never even saw the sea.
You didn't get paid, not in those days.
You had to save up for that. I remember
being on the sands every day. You know,
having a ride on a donkey, an ice cream,
that sort of thing. Never more than a week.
By and large you'd go to a boarding house,
pay for the bed but you would provide
all the eatables. Later on when
I became an adult, my own holidays,
it shows that things had improved.
'Pack your baggage and truck to me,
we'll raise Cain and a family,
living in clover, thrilling all over with love.'
I had my name down for the big firm
at the time, Metropolitan Vickers.
They called it 'the big house'. To get
in there as long as you did your work
you knew that you were set for life.
12 streets and 4 avenues due to factories
all around. We were a little nation
of our own. We were Trafford Park.
When my wife got in and had a baby come
'Bugger off to work,' they says, 'You're
in the road. We'll do better than you.'
But they'd borrow a cup of sugar or an egg.
Marvellous people, marvellous people.

IV

See where Christ's blood streams
above Manchester. Pigeons settle
in the interstices of his toes

and their dung and feathers
mottle his toenails. Flapping out
into August rain each of their pinions
resounds with the bells of his love.

Above Ancoats Hospital the box
of a cantilever crane brushes
over his hair. To the ghosts

of horses that tramp
the towing path of the Bridgewater canal
the whole of Trafford Park
gleams in his assurances,

'Here is not heaven! Here is not heaven!'
On Palatine Road Christian shifts
under his burden. Beside

one-way traffic in Newton Street
the authors of the apocryphal gospels
pause to shake out their umbrellas.
The blood of Christ mingles

with rain and mixes with detritus
from the city in the onrush
to drains. Under the streets

tunnels that sighed with boredom
hug their own hollowness.
Christ's blood streams in the firmament.
Take heed that ye clamber too high

or come too near to the brink
of the hill called Error for this
is a by-way to hell. The Pomona Docks

are neither soft nor workable.
In No. 1 a docker crushed
between a coal barge and a lighter
bleeds his marrow into the nailed palms

of the Lord. 'My Father on the Cross;
please take this anger from me
and draw me close to thee.'

CHRISTMAS ALL YEAR ROUND

I herded all these people together under the tree;
I wasn't trying to press them to anything much
but it did seem one of the continuities of the situation.
Try as they might to hold each other together
there was always someone too scared to stay silent.
Pressed against each other, some against the trunk,
and some bent under the branches, I knew something
would be blabbed out and I'd be walking off
to some hut to find something precious, or half a day
later someone would come walking into the village
with their hands tied to a bough across the neck
and I'd've done nothing more than sit under that
selfsame tree staring up at the cloud canopy
over the mountains, or gone to find chickens' eggs
from the usual places; enjoying some sensation
I'd get slung in the stockade for, back at base.
But out here I knew money was piling up
in the bank and I didn't have any family to shell
it out on, so I'd just go on hanging around,
eyeing the head man's daughter and waiting for
birds to migrate over the passes and down
the valleys; to pluck little ones from the lime.
Village kids come and rip them from the branches.
The trees are full of clumps of feathers or quails' feet
broken off at the angle. The evening fires are sweet
with flesh; their flames jitter in rainbows.
Each bird cooks differently. Their bones split
indifferently in the mouth but the pieces harbour
secret nutrients. Sometimes men come down
from the mountains to chew on whatever's left.

THE BEST MAN

I

The elephant's front foot is round and the back foot oval. The back footprint overlaps the front. You can see the way it was going from the scuffed up earth at the back.

If you learn anything about a country
from its television, then I've learned nothing here.
American programmes and other peoples' adverts.
A weather map like an empty room. Her father's
dress sense guards the family. At the wedding,
he wore one layer of hair quiffed over another,
an open-necked, blue shirt and tight blue jeans.
The servants are catatonically silent. In a country
without vacuum cleaners we were woken
by the sound of brushes up the corridor carpet.

Do you remember the Red Sea Hotel, Alison,
sending that kitten to sleep by stroking its nose?
Tomorrow night, when the new couple have taken down
their 'Do not disturb', we will come here à trois.
The same high ceilings with their turning fans;
the dance band in its uniform; bouillabaisse.
Perhaps it is the three initials sewn on the back
of each waiter's collar that stops the dancers
running up the lawn from their evening display
to serve poire belle Hélène, omelette Norwégienne.

II

Giraffes can run at up to 50 kph and between strides all four feet are off the ground. They have the largest heart of any land mammal and a valve in their necks to stop the blood rushing into their heads when they drink.

Billy's house has a big problem with snakes.
He has to kill at least one every day.
He told us of a patrol along the worn bed
of a stream; how he'd stepped up to the path,
and hear 'Mine!' echo behind him along the line.
During the war he was never directly in a contact,
but he was often around when a contact was made.
'They'd say there were three of them, two carrying
one who was badly wounded, very badly wounded.
And it was just a patch of earth to me.
But sure enough, a hundred yards ahead
was the wounded chap, and the other two
set up thirty yards on either side.
'Twenty years ago it would have been an
impertinence for a black man to speak to you in English.
You spoke to them in Chalapalapa, Kitchen Kaffir.'

A SMALL TOWN IN THE SUDAN

I

There is an autumn in the heat.
Yesterday she cut his hair in the garden,
and hair and small leaves spiralled
over the sand. In the sunset a dog
moves from heat to heat among the refuse
on a corrugated roof as she comes
from the shower wrapped in a towel
and shaking her thin wet hair.

Tonight slender girls will pass their house.
Round their heads the gaudy scarves
of black and gold, of orange and brown,
and on their heads the wicker trays.
One of them will stop outside the house
and sit beside a hurricane lamp
to winnow peanuts. He thinks that she
will do this for forty years, and that
already she will have some particular way
of twisting paper funnels, of flicking
peanuts so the least amount is lost.
His wife will dry her hair and go out
past card players under the tree –
they look up and straighten their white emmas,
their white jellabias – and she will give
the smiling girl crumpled money.

II

Out at Tiber, under the discreet racuba,
a white boy rucks up inside the bint al tahour.
He thinks of the fly scrabbling inside
a windscreen, a fly drowning in an unwashed pan,
his pen scrambling on the page of his diary.

III

'Syrians have been here for a hundred years.'
Their women come to the cathedral,
with lowered eyes, and stockinged bandy legs
and stand among dusty leggy Dinka boys.
Their men bring in the smell of shaving water,
sweat and cheap perfume. And in their neat,
clean shirts they give a pound to each child,
and take ten themselves, to the collection box.
They feel they pay too much and never enough,
for children who lie on the floor and clap,
to nuns who stare and cajole. 'They're so inbred,
there's always one in every family.'

IV

'We have a guava tree that gives
one fruit a week if we can save it
from the ants. Every morning we look
in our socks and the ants shiver round
the hole down which we let the poison.
One day the World Service brought us
the voices of Vietnamese in Ulster,
voices coloured with the Ulster vowels.
I did not consider that real, the hours
of quiet in the afternoon, or the English classrooms
I had left, or us together on the last flight home.'

FELLOW TRAVELLERS

The train begins our slow drift back
down through the boney mountains
to the cultivation of the valley floor.

Perhaps she feels herself a widow already,
clutching narcissi to her half-open coat,
and staring through the window,

like Sharaku's actor staring at the priest.
Perhaps there is a map among the trees.
In the stillness of the bird's head

is the movement of the stem it holds.
I lent boots to her quiet husband
and we crossed the fields to visit

the baptistry window: three hares
that dance endlessly in a circle,
and iron nails twisted in a crucifix,

the naked, halting fire of the man beneath;
to handle the book as if it was his own,
as if the marks there were made by him.

AN APPROXIMATION

A lightness is travelling towards you
as if towards a sweetheart; you frown
at the rush of air and run your fingers

over the brickwork as darkness calls
from the shelter below to that sudden
absence of dark when burnt air

folds around you and your ears pop
into silence. Nothing, not even
the mute presence of angels,

will ever take away the blinding light
rushing up from inside you.
The sun rises in silence;

a fractured pipe gushes water
over your sock. A wall has fallen
over the doll your uncle brought back

from Delancey; its hair is rubbishy
with dust. In twenty years
how will the spiders choose between

the furry bags of dead flies? A yacht
is anchored in morning sun as the sea
opens onto nowhere and onto nothing.

*

In the bed a man and woman lie
back to back. She is reading.
The pastel coloured duvet plumps out

the acreage of bed. She turns a page.
In the tallboy the woman's clothes
are bundled and crushed; the man's

are piled in plastic wrapping.
Coils of clothes and collars
stiff in packets. Surfaces

collect in Chinese boxes;
the attack upon Lodh airport,
a pile of breeze blocks, an answer

from the angle-poise lamp.
They do not show how the lines
from a wagging tail, or dragging foot,

run concurrently over the frozen canal;
or how, pushing his stick into mud
for support, he knows the print

of each new disturbance, the way
the grass lies with the pulse
of ice clouded by slackening breath.

*

B. 52's above the desert tense
the line of coast; where blocks
of flats hold expat nurses;

the long drive down the coast road
to the Emirates. Lights dance
upon hands of pilots,

a projectile enters sand,
and flame and world
climb upon themselves.

Windows buckle in the radio car.
All of Whitehall pauses
in the snow; there is skidding,

policemen run at full stretch.
The horse guards' horses sing.
A tourist stands there

while he can. Taxi drivers
pause to grab some lunch.
I queue for sandwiches myself.

*

In the sunset newsmen
by the International Hotel
file their news on camera.

Lights on tripods turn
upon a man in a bomber jacket,
as the soundman in his headphones

holds up the microphone. Beyond
the airport and across a headland
seagrass grazing dugongs

are not so far below the surface.
When the kingfish leapt as the man
walked into the sea, it seemed

to train its eye on him; a parabola
neatly timed in air and light.
Down from the mint blue mosque

small birds skitter over the beach;
and cormorants flap smoothly
or glide along the coast.

*

Trees grow up stoney hillside
and an organ plays
to an empty church;

the cat is spreading
on a Christmas sweater,
as flamingos ribbon up the Gulf.

A captive bird loses twenty-five percent
of bone weight in its lifetime.
Osteoporosis, usually confined

to women over fifty, thrives in zoos.
What the average dugong needs
is sixty years of history.

*

Turtles and the moon drag
up the beach; sun and men
stand on the quay. Inside

an A.P.C. waves break, the barrel
of a gun paints a trajectory.
A lorry crosses onto a bridge;

a bridge held in a minute and lost
in a second with the driver's spine
and fourteen droopy eared sheep.

You, with your muddy distasha
rusty Kalashnikov,
and flip-flops, take

your rhino-hide whip,
pull up your camel and look
down into the Euphrates.

*

Silent and out of place,
I think of a whole population;
a Victorian world preserved

around me as I sit with
my own time concealed
on video, and on the bookshelves.

Beyond me is the semi-desert,
F. 15's peel back the fabric
of sky. The sun shapes

turrets and adobe houses
into Downham Market and Swaffham.
The children hold each other

through the Fens from Cambridge
onto Lincoln, where the car drives
into the shadow of the only hill

for thirty miles; the Cathedral close,
the still canals, other children
born beside them. The Fens

discourse among themselves.
A time-line drawn from bargee
to tank commander is a line

most powerfully straight,
uncontaminated by the pull
of the moon, as eels drawn

to Fenland drains swim
among drowned tanks,
and sunken F. 15's.

THE GLASS ENCLOSURE

I

Let us dismantle the sound,
the smell of musty crêpe-de-Chine,
armpits and unclean arses,
sweat mixed with 'Nina Ricci'
shuffle such cards as there are,

bend them into a chorus
of dismay and let them flutter out
over an inland sea. You should know
I was a bagman too, ran
my fingers along the edges

of those fanned cards
and when the car ran over
black ice and George Wilkerson died
and Ernie Daniels had his ribs
caved in, I collected on

the insurance, spread out
the cards, bought a No. 5 reed,
ran my fingers over major ninths,
and thirteenths, felt
the lines in two times at once,

looked over the balcony,
nearly spat on his head,
put my fingers where I thought
they should go and where I thought
I could change things I did;

I blew a column of air with no sound,
asked him what I could,
and got no reply from the man
beside the chicken hut
whose records I slowed down,

whose grooves I filled with dust
learning the correct fingering
from Tommy Douglas, poor bastard,
who knew what he was doing
so well they wouldn't let him hear

a white orchestra, so we sat
from sixty-second tune
to sixty-second tune and then
I finally did it, stood up,
played into the middle eight,

pushed into double time, dragged
the drummer with me as Tommy
became a memory and the pack
of chords spread up into the air
and kept on falling, falling.

II

What is a train but a place to die in?
The dazzlement of the small time song
and dance man twinkles on an open blade

with the lights from passing towns
poised above her shoulder. Badly embalmed
he looked just as I remembered him;

caked in pan, an accompanist for sudden strippers
in tough spots. Beauty is power made visible;
He walked up to the music for the last time

as if he had heard it all before. The man
who trails wires from the john to the bandstand –
creases upon a pair of hound's-tooth trousers,

hands upon the handrail – stops recording
the moment I take the horn from my mouth.
Everybody wants to hear what I've done;

nobody wants to hear what I'm doing.
A house upon a firm footing and us living the life
of Reilly in every room catching the light

of a louvred window like the sound of a dog
barking, the tune stolen, inverted and then
played so we all know where we are.

'Let's play the National Anthem, gentlemen.
I think you can all play that.' A skull
cracked open by a night-stick is left all night

in a police cell until its mother comes
to collect it the next morning and the life
that follows; early evening walking with the wife;

these things fall under the fingers, control
the breath. The beating heart contrives
a glass enclosure; a dance around the grave,

a hollow stick, a strand from a horse's tail
and finally round the rich cembalo;
the train getting nearer, tricky-tracking past.

III

Another valley; an arena
of air triangulated
from the same point
in different hands.

The different player; below
another view, where practice
lends a shape to the air
like cloud crossing.

Do anything, something;
rather than fill the room,
clench the heart,
and wrap up ideas.

The spread of silence;
check the reed
and oil keys to toss
a hat into this ring.

The staves gesticulate;
the music runs ahead;
one note tupping the next
leads us somewhere else.

An ante-bellum mansion;
they dance the Lindy-hop
with the history of European music
snapping at their heels.

IV

Am I still dancing on the head of a pin?
I slip into the spaces made by others
and look down at my own fingers.

Stubby, virile, acrid, I'd swear they were
possessed. I feel a fluttering on my cheek.
In the spaces, faces moon up at me

from the rail-tracks of my arms. A decent suit
can't keep my feet upon the ground.
When I upset people, I feel the other cheek

burning and long for an angel breeze
to cool it down, for tiny feet to cling
to my shoulders. I know that all this

is a prayer. However much I try,
I'll encounter all the wreckage of religion
when I die. I should have fired them

when they told that poor boy not to play;
vaselining the cork joints on his clarinet.
They are fighting round my legacy

before my time. I've tried enough.
I want to write in one voice; to take
gravity and hold the moment

when the panels fold towards me.
I'll paint the outside stairs
and help with small domestic expenses.

Once I had a friend who died. He had
a feeling for the hysteria of the times.
Was I an angel from the very start?

My mother got a one-party phone
and brought up my son. At the club
they had every kind of bird but forgot

to book the mynah; it would have drenched
in nicotine and flapped and called
through all the solos, 'Does God still speak to man?'

V

Where was his horn on the day he died?
That girl came with a man she remembered.
The girl's hair so fiery it looked about
to catch fire; yellow moccasins, pink
sweater. She said, 'When I married him

all he had was a horn and a habit.
He gave me the habit so I might
as well have the horn.' He wanted
to be put in a burlap bag, but he was
put away as nice as anyone had seen.

It is a shock this house. The windows
blown out, the fire escape hanging loudly
from a wall; but there is yarrow,
bayberry still dropped with fruit
and the worn patch of grass

where we have all stood to wonder
at the ceiling collapsing on the room
below and the person who has not
waited there. 'They wanted me to pay
but this place was named after me.

There isn't anybody a big shot;
the boys don't drink – they're not
on speaking terms with the devil.
But working this way is like undressing
a girl. Each layer a garment. First,

the rough woollies, then the delicate silk.'
He hummed a few bars of Orange
was the Colour of her Dress then Blue Silk.
So time stunned itself in that house,
and the man who lived there learned

not to wait for friends to call with a beer
and reproaches for not having been
at the game. He sat for a while
in the sun then picked up his horn and went
inside to practise Body and Soul in F sharp.

AUNT

There've been three suicides in the village
since I've been here. Dave, who took the pub,
walked down to the river at four in the morning
with a gun. The same day she had another man
in her bed, and put it about that he'd been
sleeping with his daughter. I don't believe it.
Two more normal teenagers you couldn't wish
to meet and the next week the boy put his hand

through a plate glass window. The house
opposite Mrs Akerill's stall that we saw
this afternoon; Mr Barrell, Bernard Barrell,
he was so depressed when he was made redundant
he took his car up to the main road.
He left a note for his little girl, for when
she came home from school, telling her
where to find him, his wife was out at work.

Then Mick, you know Mick, from the house,
not next door, but two doors down,
his mother walked out on his father.
They all have guns, beautiful guns,
the gun clubs are very strong round here
and his father went and shot himself
in the churchyard. Here, have half of this
with me.
Icing sugar falls around her feet.

THE QUIET LIMITS

Lights swung from side
to side and mist settled
over the window where light
was calling on my skin.

I walked out into the shadow
of the church tower. I hold on
to things more satisfactorily
than you think; that moment

when the car kicks tram rails
and wrists give way. Then,
when you check the mirror,
the hand patting hair is yours.

THERAPIES

to Jean Forshaw

It occurred to me when talking to you;
visitors through the front gate,
she with her short blond hair,

and he, it seems like short blond hair
at this distance, and you said, Stay with that,
will you? then voices at the end

of the corridor and the dark of the front room,
silence and the traffic in the street;
after you had sent them away you returned

and sat down with the pad on your knee,
all that in the time it took them to reach
the front gate, I saw her turn to him

and give him that look which said;
We've been sent away, and, What a strange woman,
Isn't she the Vicar's wife? then back out

of the gate, us left in the front room
as I tried to stay with it,
the dark room, the dull day outside.

AN ABIDING INTEREST

I DECORATING

'Just cleaning up streets' Peter Sutcliffe

I hear my footsteps on the beach.
Beside me is the memory of women
in Chapeltown; their blood is dried
upon the paintbrush of our time.

On the flattened end of the screwdriver,
that they will always hear knocking carefully
inside a jam jar, are girls' names
wiped upon the faintly scented handkerchief

his wife had ironed on the nights
when he was out, hearing the cries
of gulls, feeling the sea breezes,
and the pebbles sliding underfoot.

II CAIN

I saw limes reach through green
to yellow and apples began
to pick themselves. My hands

stiffened round the ropes but not
one furrow packed against another;
no robins, nor greasy ends

of broken worms over the shards
of the third day. My calloused heels
were cracked and micropore peeled off

into turning earth. The horizons
filled with sheep. I saw burning swords
unsheathed by cherubim and eyes

like owls' eyes in the sheeps' heads.
Lamps were chasing night
over the moor and police cars spread

through Saddleworth. Those tapes
of him grunting through squat thrusts
and weights tumbling in bloody heaps.

III DENNIS

My cousin by adoption killed himself last week.
It appears that he'd been knocking off this woman and,
the previous week, her husband had beaten him up.

I can't have met him now for going on
for twenty years but as a child I often went
to Aunty Vera's house in Park View Road.

My Uncle Frank cycled home each day from Bull Motors.
At the end of his life he pedalled round the house
with Parkinson's Disease and kept on falling off.

I thought I knew my cousins well; always having
to play their games, calling turds 'jolly-lollies',
their terraced other-side-of-Ipswich life.

My cousin had been a gifted trumpeter
and won a place at Kneller Hall but turned it
down to play at the Sebastopol each week.

He had become a Special Constable and after
Ipswich versus Middlesbrough on Boxing Day
he drove off, parked the car beside the A45,

and threw himself from the Orwell Bridge.
Either he misjudged it or he judged it well
and avoided landing in the river with its possibility

of life and hit a field one hundred and fifty feet
below. I have often thought of suicide
but now he knows what I will never know;

that first attempt to fly, the air filling out
his uniform and passing like water
through his fingers, that sudden, painless stop;

and perhaps, earlier that day, he heard
the swaying crowd at Portman Road, like one
gigantic Siamese twin, shouting out his name, DENNNNIIIISSS.

THE SAME CONDEMNATION

There were not too many of us, I always felt
and I was always so glad of that,
that there were never too many of us.
It did, for example, at the very least,
grant an uninterrupted view of the river.

A crane like a single spider's leg.
And I imagine a man climbing
to the cab of the crane would wonder,
when he returned to earth, where was the earth.
And I never had the feeling, if I may use

so prosaic an image, of being the torn half
of a bus ticket, as I would surely have done
had there been more of us, and less uncertainty.
I have always found in my dealings with you
that a certain uncertainty has led

to a feeling of closer acquaintanceship;
a rather British feeling, one suspects,
in this day and age. And one that,
I hasten to add, I could not have shared
with the others. Not that they were

insensitive men; they were, each in his own way,
the very milk of human kindness,
whatever one might have read to the contrary,
and later. But uncertainty was their stock-in-trade
as it were, whereas I am, and always

have been, a rather nervous man.
susceptible always to the firm handshake,
the misted car, to Norrie's moments
for lightening the atmosphere, as much as
I recognised how that irritated James.

Huddled, as in a rainy bus-shelter,
amidst these uncertain friends, you yearn,
like the landlord's dog, for comfort.
And when the comfort of events was set
in train, I imagined us a set of boys

catching the bus to town, on a Saturday morning,
ground cigarette ash, bus breath
already half a morning used (my father
'Some of us work on Saturdays, you know.')
and further up the cambered top deck of the bus,

a single woollen glove. As it was,
these pictures were not too far from the truth.
For when we left the pub, they in their car,
we in ours, I had, as I have had before,
and dare say will again, a feeling

of running above the common-mill of things
as if I too sang in the outermost branches.
And this was so even as we crossed,
and recrossed, the soft illogical river,
to wait beside a lorry in a lay-by, its engine running.

GIFTS

We hold the eyelids down; dress
to fetch the midwife from four doors
down the same row of privvies;
we use a sharp garland of words;
entry, snicket, alley and back.

To come in and out, to dress
a plain body on a plain bed
to soften and to fold in tissue,
dealt with by the cheque book
and the decent, kindly word, to seal

artifacts with the body; a picture,
teddy bears, rattles and ribbons
closed and fading under glass,
where smokey flames float on oil,
and every Sunday changes the flowers.

Take flowers or a plant to the host,
not those peculiar biscuits
laid on window shelves for weeks
to smell of honey and dust; turning
flesh to stone and stone to words.

A LOCAL SENSE

I PARK VIEW ROAD

Light clung to umbrellas
in the studio. She wore
her hair up and a mohair jumper

and I had my hand upon her shoulder.
In our mother's bungalow
that photo stands upon the wooden box

of cutlery my sister also gave.
Behind the Inkerman the bowling green
was always empty. Click, click,

went the pub sign. Four chestnut trees
with just bare earth beneath them
stood beside the A12.

In rubberised cowboy suits
the landlord's son and I
threw sticks into the leaves.

Sometimes chestnuts dropped
like broadbeans from their velvet.
Girls who lived in our road

grew long legs and left.
Two of them played records
for the half-time crowd

at Portman Road. Under
an elder bush Angela and I
agreed to marry. Ten years later,

when I'd come off a Vespa
and smashed my ankle, she was nursing
in the hospital but I could not speak.

I was clinically bored;
the St John's ambulance man,
I'd crashed beside, who tied my legs

together before he picked me
off the road, came to see me
in the ward. I simply sat and stared.

II HUMBER DOUCY LANE

I collected up the windfalls and packed them
in a cupboard for the winter. They didn't keep
the taut smell of bark and musty autumn

but shrivelled and yellowed like the tapes
put round the trees to trap caterpillars
that climbed the trunks. I cut-out

the middleman, took the fruit to grocers'
in the precinct and put a notice
on our gate. Mother said that I could

keep the money. But no-one came to buy.
In my shed, fifty yards from the house,
dried spiders and a drumkit replaced

the chemist's bench and tubes; gas-jars
I brewed oxygen in to flare magnesium strips;
the whole hut and the orchard brightened.

As instructed by my teachers I turned
my head away. Years afterwards, our neighbour,
Mrs Johnson, splintery with Alzheimer's,

walked naked up and down the lane. Her labrador pup,
hit a glancing blow by a car on Rushmere Road,
pulled weakly from his basket to lick my face.

III MAVILI STREET

Since, at fifteen, you had driven
fifty yards I now sat
clutching you as we drove
the silence of valleys

down to the shoreline.
Under olive trees nets were spread
to catch the falling fruit. Families
pruned branches into fires.

Away from the exhausts we smelled
the olive's sweet, blue drift.
I didn't often see beyond
a milk of ouzo and ice.

When I left you changed
the hand-written name plate
that announced our dusty flat,
from 'Ian and Alison' to 'Peek'.

IV REZAYAT MOTEL

The trees survive their gardeners' guesses;
the cut white branches hang
upon the wall; sunbeds rest
on fallen, plastic leaves.

Socks and underwear, mats for pets
catch on trees. They grow
beside sunbathers' jokes,
a lazy wall, a house, a pile of bricks.

Night after night, the gardeners
queue at the post office
to remit money. Our teaboy
hasn't seen his wife in three years;

has a daughter over two years old.
I pick up stones to ward off strays,
and walk sand-driven alleys
over to a neighbouring compound.

V ANDREWS BUILDINGS

Three times in the weekend
I visit the baker's; sesame rolls
bloom in the palm of my hand.
At the dry-cleaner's I admire
the varnish of wrapping

clinging to a jacket.
In the picture framer's
one colour placed upon another
rises like roofs of Land Rovers
above dry-stone walls.

Sheep turn and bite tics
in curlicues of fleece. Grass
or snow, sheep are picked out
on the field. My step-son
runs back from his school,

and in his head he scythes
his enemies with his school bag;
fallen like forty goats
the village had in 1926;
like the curate and his five chickens.

VI AT THE NAVIGATION

The sun was tucked behind the visor
as I was driving back from work;
the road reached round from house

to house. A horse was grazing
an out-of-season cricket pitch.
They were leading sheep down

to the reservoir; hooves slipped
from bank to crumpled sky; fleecy heads
bobbed out towards the middle.

Parish boundaries widen
every year; another heart attack,
another priest who's irreplaceable,

whose altar glides to silence.
And half a mile below the crinkly spine
of England, a couple leg their boat

and feel, from the neighbouring tunnel,
the pulse of a train tearing
towards the whole of Europe.

FOR JON, PAM, TOM AND KATIE UP IN THE AIR

I

So what did you think with Katie on your knee
as the plane turned in over the Harbour?
That tame dolphins are not the same as piccolos;

that as it was in the beginning, is now,
and ever shall be; that the prickling at the roots
of your hair is the light dancing from the waves

in Hong Kong Harbour, like buttons on a radio,
and not the jackhammer of the heart above the baby
sleeping on your knee or the song you never heard;

'The Danger Zone' that Ray Charles sang throughout
the Cuban missile crisis? And does she think the knee
she lies on is the bell of a sackbut or a crumhorn

and the air is turning in a harmony? Another body
is hoisted under the sun onto the catafalque
of a cargo container amongst other rusting metal.

The men beat their heads and chests and tread
the ground into hysteria. The women ululate.
A military helicopter waits overhead. A fire engine

sprays the black crowd tautening among the hills
of the northwest of the city. Strung with lights
and tannoys, the integuments of the half-built blocks

and electricity substations whisper the dry earth
spooned out, passed among the crowd and eaten.
Smoke and fog copulate around the arms of the Buddha,

and Pam's plane lowers over the warm, cut stone.
Crew cut DJs play the clean cut music;
Chet Baker and Gerry Mulligan played a negro music

in the West Coast Cool School fashion till Chet
was grabbed and stomped on so his lips
fed back inside his teeth and all the notes

that blew were blown inside his head.
Heat and the exhaust smooth down the runway
and bear the planes and birds back into the sky.

II

Here, there is no memory palace;
no warriors locked in combat
in the southeast corner
of the reception hall;

in the northeast corner
there is no Xixia woman
who is huihui. Only this
that after the plane had rolled

to a stop, the faces in the aisles
with bags, brushes and hoovers,
busy in the toilets, recapping
hand lotion, washing toilet bowls.

And in their memory palace?
A crown prince at the gaming tables.
That all that is farang and this
is what we keep even to ourselves,

unless we trust the farang
with the most precious things
that are not theirs and can
only be trusted with them.

*

'Let us take a tuk-tuk into the foul air.'
So Jenny leaping from the chair
she sat in. The children in the hotel care.

Their sleep is smuggling down the intercom.
The hotel nurse who looks just twelve
with ten years in the Gulf and lucky

still to be alive. Like us as we pitch
on three wheels from Soi Carboy to Patpong
and clutch each other even tighter.

English – off to where the girls smoke
cigarettes with their vaginas and then blow
paper darts through cardboard tubes.

'It was like being hypnotised. He showed me
a piece of silk I didn't really want
and couldn't afford. Then he did

that draping bit and started telling me
what it did for my eyes and my hair
and the next thing I knew, I was out

on the street with three and a half yards
of the damned stuff.' A house
with walls turned inside out

so the carvings face the diners.
And where is the ivory mouse palace?
Somewhere up the stairs and on the left.

*

And if something terrible happens,
something not unlike a sudden,
mighty wind, Simonides, among
the passengers, will remember

the exact positions of the relatives
and friends, aisle or window,
as his eye blinks the cursor;
business class, smoking.

For here, in the toilet of the memory
palace, the hand lotion is finally
uncapped and its pink lines run along
the toilet walls and across the ceiling.

III

Leaping over the Pearl River
cost him a broken ankle
and a limp for the rest
of his days; catching the metro
took a minute, two dollars
and enough left for another pair

of cloisonne vases.
The world's longest escalator
takes you well away
from screaming Boat People
and wet ropes slopping wood.
Children of six and seven

play inside the Walled City;
no more walled than you or I.
'I mean, it was a million
to one chance we'd walk past
that shop again and then
she dashed out to tell me

she'd been through the whole shop
and found the matching one.
And so, after that, I had to buy it.'
Wet hawsers slap the Walled City.
It pitches in its own mind,
yawing through the forty-five degrees

of the spirits of its ancestors.
Lines of washing slide from balconies
toward the loosening horizon.
Sixty-six stitches cross his back
and hold together the zany ideogram
of his knife wounds. Girls

and their numbers are chosen
by the customers through the grill.
All of them slip a little further
into kilter and the permanent rain;
a splinter of bone that pierced
the right kneecap. As they attached

a metal brace to stop his right leg
shrivelling shorter than his left,
a vision of Mary and her child
left his heart serene and his flesh
finally untroubled by lust.
Ropes tighten into the sea;

and all of Aberdeen twinkles at night
from the top of the world's longest
escalator until it takes the rapids
at full sail and in a moment
is turned over and spun round
along with two other ships

in which are travelling
the mandarin's possessions.
Thus did I and João Barradas
get sent to the Bottom. But God
aided me because I caught hold
of some Rope which by Divine

Providence I found between my Hands
and was able to pull myself
onto a Support of the same Ship.
But João Barradas went to the Bottom
and the Current carried him away
and he never reappeared.

IV

It was the pecking of a single bird that made
the hardened ground throw up all of this;

the car tracks and the stiffened marks of rain.
From reed beds threaded with the empty cans

and plastic cups, the koala yawns up
into old light and shakes off the dust.

He remembers pissing on the Minister of Tourism
just a week before they handed him to Tom

and lurches off into the untravelled, unnamed
nothing. Both he and Cook create the space

that runs between the verses. There is no name
without a place. We'll leave most of that

to Mr Hawkesworth and the Endeavour journals;
their genius for the matter of fact and to those

who followed Cook; always filling in,
always disappointed, consecrating

a system of differences in the idea of land.
And that was only the third car between

here and Dubbo and I thought, Poor sister,
poor sister. The tennis court run to earth.

The fly screen round the verandah all
shot through; the team house left

to the visiting team. But the two rooms
where they lived she kept them very clean.

Flowers more architectural than pretty.
The continent had shut its shell before

the songlines crossed the Torres strait.
The rivers run to nothing. Casuarinas

mesh the sun. Sea wasps love us all.
The world's largest stone. Two-thirds

below the ground though how would you know?
Thousands camped there – you wouldn't notice.

All the rangers have gone walkabout.
Rod Padgett – paid for the gallery himself

and never got that back. The art shops
gave them materials and never got that back.

The couple split up. The woman went
to Perth was the better artist. Remember,

they're less than one percent of the population.
In front of the marble mausoleum the men

shiver and weep on the first anniversary.
And in a souk she has known for thirty years

a perfect stranger comes to tell her,
'Mrs Mann. I'm very sorry. Your husband

is dead.' So with the eucalyptus mist
of the Blue Mountains scented with urine,

and with a stock of dialects from Narragin
to Wearside, Tom and the koala clutch

a boomerang and a cabbage tree hat, turn
to slam the kitchen door and go back in.

NOTES

THE BIG HOUSE

I 'As I spake . . . myself alone,' Deuteronomy 1, v.9
'A bad site . . . strange styles' quoted by Pevsner in his *Buildings of England: South Lancashire*, Penguin, 1969.
II Various sources including: Bill Williams, *The Making of Manchester Jewry: 1740-1875*, Manchester University Press, 1985; Louis Golding, *Magnolia Street*, Gollancz, 1932; recorded oral testimonies in Manchester Jewish Museum, and the anonymous ballad 'Hugh of Lincoln'.
III 'Dahrendorf on Britain' part two, broadcast on BBC Television.
IV 'Take heed that ... by-way to hell' John Bunyan, *Pilgrims Progress*

THE BEST MAN

'The elephant's front . . . at the back.' and 'Giraffes can run . . . when they drink.'; tour guide, Wanke Game Reserve, Zimbabwe, 1988.

A SMALL TOWN IN THE SUDAN

emma: a white cloth wound around the head, *jellabiya*: a white robe, *racuba*: a reed shelter, or lean-to, *bint al tahour*: a circumcised girl, *Dinka*: a Southern Sudanese tribe.

THE GLASS ENCLOSURE

The title is taken from a composition of the same name by the American jazz pianist and composer, Bud Powell. Certain details in this poem have been freely adapted from accounts of the lives of Bud Powell and Charlie Parker. I am indebted to Ross Russell's biography of Parker *Bird Lives*, Quartet, 1973.
'. . . an accompanist for sudden strippers in tough spots.' Roy Fisher.
'Beauty is power made visible.' Eric Gill.
'Everybody wants to hear what I've done; nobody wants to hear what I'm doing.' John Coltrane.

THE SAME CONDEMNATION

'And one of the malefactors which were hanged railed on him,
saying, If thou be Christ, save thyself and us'.
'But the other answering rebuked him, saying, Dost not thou fear
God, seeing thou are in the same condemnations'. *St. Luke 23, 39-40.*

FOR JON, PAM, TOM AND KATIE UP IN THE AIR

II Some details are taken from Jonathan D. Spence, *The Memory Palace of Matteo Ricci*, Faber, 1985.

III As above, part II; Spence, op.cit., plus a photo essay on Hong Kong in *Granta*.

IV Some details taken from Paul Carter, *The Road to Botany Bay*, Faber, 1987.

IAN POPLE was born in Ipswich and educated at the British Council, Athens and the universities of Aston and Manchester. He has taught English in secondary and higher education in Sudan, Greece, Saudi Arabia and Britain. He is married to the novelist Livi Michael and lives in Saddleworth, with his wife and two sons.